My Psychotherapy Journal

My Psychotherapy Journal

◆

Psychological healing & growth through journaling

J. Slava Thaler

iUniverse, Inc.

New York Lincoln Shanghai

My Psychotherapy Journal
Psychological healing & growth through journaling

iUniverse, Inc.

For information address:
iUniverse, Inc.
2021 Pine Lake Road, Suite 100
Lincoln, NE 68512
www.iuniverse.com

By reading and/or using this book, you agree that this book is meant only as a resource and **not** as a substitute for seeking help from a mental health professional. The reader further agrees not to hold the author liable for any problems or damages that arise from direct or indirect use of this resource.

ISBN: 0-595-30857-0

Printed in the United States of America

Contents

Introduction

Psychotherapy is a collaborative process of psychological healing and growth. As you embark on this process, keeping a journal can help you:

- Keep track of key learnings and what is happening in your therapy.
- Set therapy goals for yourself.
- See your progress in therapy.

Keeping a journal can also be a therapeutic process in itself; your journal can become an additional "therapist", allowing you to:

- Write out difficult feelings and thoughts that you don't feel comfortable speaking yet.
- Become more responsible for your own therapy.
- Work out smaller issues that arise between therapy sessions through journaling.
- Work out larger issues, using your journal as well as your therapist. By using this journal once before your therapy session and once afterward, you are receiving 3 therapy sessions "for the price of one"!

Important note : please make your therapist aware that you are using a psychotherapy journal. Sometimes this journaling process uncovers deep feelings and issues that may necessitate a more immediate conversation or visit to your therapist, or another psychological professional.

My Psychotherapy Journal covers 20 therapy sessions. The journal assumes that you are going to a therapy session (individual, group, couples, and/or family) approximately once a week; if you are seeing a therapist more often simply find a journaling duration that works best for you (either journaling every session, or every week). If your therapy is shorter than 20 sessions, you may continue journaling after your therapy is over, answering the journaling questions most relevant to you. If your therapy is longer than 20 sessions, you may either continue journaling in a notebook, or purchase another copy of *My Psychotherapy Journal* to use in the rest of your psychotherapy sessions.

Each section of *My Psychotherapy Journal* incorporates a relevant quote. This section's quote is:

"I have found power in the mysteries of thought"—Euripides

Prior to 1st session

In meeting a therapist for the first time, you will need to decide whether:

1. There is rapport and trust between you and the therapist, and

2. Whether the therapist can help you with your problem(s).

Take some time to think about the following questions. Please note that when writing out answers to these questions (and to all other questions) in this book, they don't need to be perfect! This is not a test, the answers are not written in stone (you can always go back and change what you wrote), and unless you choose otherwise, nobody else needs to see this book. (It is strongly recommended to share insights gleamed from this process with your therapist, but whether or not you want to share the entire book is up to you.)

What are some qualities I look for in a trusting relationship? (If you need more space to answer this question, or any other question in this journal, feel free to write in the margins or on a separate sheet of paper.)

_____

_____

_____

_____

_____

How do I know that I trust someone?

_____

_____

_____

_____

_____

How do I know that someone trusts me?

_____

_____

_____

_____

_____

What are some qualities I look for in a person that I like?

_____

_____

_____

_____

_____

What are the problems for which I am seeking therapy?

_____

_____

_____

_____

_____

On a scale of 1 (lowest) to 5 (highest), how *ready* do I feel to change in order to overcome these problems?

1   2   3   4   5

On a scale of 1 (lowest) to 5 (highest), how *motivated* do I feel to change in order to overcome these problems?

1   2   3   4   5

"Love all, trust a few. Do wrong to none."—William Shakespeare

After 1st session

To make this journal most valuable to you, please respond to the first 3 "after the session" section statements within one or two days of your therapy session. If you have a tendency to procrastinate, consider answering these three questions in the waiting room to your therapist's office after your therapy session.

What we talked about in our therapy session:

_____

_____

_____

_____

_____

Main items or ideas that stand out from today's session:

_____

_____

_____

_____

_____

Key things I need to work on this week include:

_____

_____

_____

_____

_____

In choosing whether this therapist is a good fit for you, answer the following two questions:

1. Do I feel a rapport and trust between the therapist and myself?

_____

_____

_____

_____

_____

2. Do I feel that this therapist can help me with my problem(s)?

_____

_____

_____

_____

_____

Some people are able to answer these questions after one session, while others need several sessions to decide these questions. If you need more time, answer these two questions again after the next two sessions.

If you have decided *not* to work with this therapist, simply update the "Prior to 1st session" before seeing your next therapist, and this "After 1st session" after seeing your next therapist. Repeat until you find a therapist that suits you.

If you have decided to work with this therapist, simply continue with this journal.

"I know God will not give me anything I can't handle. I just wish that He didn't trust me so much."–Mother Theresa

Prior to 2nd session

Dreams are one way of the mind symbolically moving thoughts or emotions from unconscious to being conscious. As you go through therapy, dreams are an important way of getting "in tune" with your unconscious thoughts, feelings, and desires. To make this journal most valuable to you, keep it by your bedside and write down every dream that you have from now until the end of your therapy experience. Below you will find some space to write out two dreams, then a larger blank space in which you can fill out as many other dreams as you have. If you do not remember your dreams yet that is ok, you will start remembering them when the time is right for you.

First dream

_____

_____

_____

_____

_____

How I felt upon waking from this dream (this is the "feelings" purpose of your dream):

Second dream

_____

_____

_____

_____

How I felt upon waking from this dream:

Other dreams (remember to also write how you felt upon waking from each dream).

_____

_____

_____

_____

_____

Now shift to the problem(s) that you are working on in therapy. Write out how you are doing with those problem(s) this week.

_____

_____

_____

_____

_____

On a scale of 1 (lowest) to 5 (highest), how *ready* do I feel to change in order to overcome these problems?

1   2   3   4   5

On a scale of 1 (lowest) to 5 (highest), how *motivated* do I feel to change in order to overcome these problems?

1   2   3   4   5

Some things that I want to cover with my therapist in our next session. These can be related to the main reason(s) you are going to therapy, other issue(s), or something completely unrelated about which you would like to speak to your therapist.

_____

_____

_____

_____

_____

"Trust in dreams, for in them is the hidden gate to eternity."—Kahill Gibran

I am so mad. Words can not describe how I feel. Why am I still fighting (trying) why don't I just quit. Haven't I been trying my whole life + look where its gotten me. I have made many poor choices + I have rebelled. So now I have been trusting in you + I believe that I'm on the path that you have set before me. I'm going no where fast but that's not your way that's mine. So now we are doing things your way. I'm to trust in you + no one else including myself. You know what I have been thinking + I haven't thought that way seller for a long time but when I was young it was constantly on my mind. I'd go back to the hospital but there is no help there you are my only hope. Where are you?

After 2nd session

What we talked about in our therapy session:

_____
_____
_____
_____
_____

Main items or ideas that stand out from today's session:

_____
_____
_____
_____
_____

Key things I need to work on this week include:

_____
_____
_____
_____
_____

Take a moment to rate [on a scale of 1 (very low), 5 (neutral), to 10 (optimal)] how you are feelings about the following five main areas of life after your therapy session.

1. Work. This includes your job or career (or education, if you are a student). This area also includes housework and volunteer work.

   a. Leisure. This includes things that you do outside of work that you enjoy.

2. Social. This includes relationships with friends and associates.

3. Sexual. This area includes how you feel about intimacy, intimate relationships which you have (if applicable), as well as how you view and feel about your own sexuality.

4. Being with yourself. This area includes how you view yourself, how well you "know yourself", and how you enjoy spending time with yourself.

5. Spirituality. This includes how you view God or a higher power and how you interact with that being. If you are agnostic or atheist, this area covers how you view spirituality or the Cosmos.

Work
1   2   3   4   5   6   7   8   9   10
(low)   (neutral)   (optimal)

Leisure

1   2   3   4   5   6   7   8   9   10

Social

1   2   3   4   5   6   7   8   9   10

Sexual

1   2   3   4   5   6   7   8   9   10

Being with myself

1   2   3   4   5   6   7   8   9   10

Spirituality

1   2   3   4   5   6   7   8   9   10

"Everyone has his [or her] own specific vocation or mission in life; everyone must carry out a concrete assignment that demands fulfillment. Therein he [or she] cannot be replaced, nor can his life be repeated, thus, everyone's task is unique as his [or her] specific opportunity to implement it."—Dr. Viktor Frankl

Prior to 3rd session

Dreams I had this week (remember to also write how you felt upon waking from each dream).

_____

_____

_____

_____

_____

Outside of your therapist's office you may notice a connection between experiences you have (or things you do), and specific lessons you learn about yourself and/or your problem(s). Keep track of such experiences and write about them here.

_____

_____

_____

_____

_____

Take some time to think about your life in general. Write about how it is changing now that you are in therapy.

_____

_____

_____

_____

_____

Now shift to the problem(s) that you are working on in therapy. Write out how you are doing with those problem(s) this week.

_____

_____

_____

_____

_____

On a scale of 1 (lowest) to 5 (highest), how *ready* do I feel to change in order to overcome these problems?

1   2   3   4   5

On a scale of 1 (lowest) to 5 (highest), how *motivated* do I feel to change in order to overcome these problems?

1   2   3   4   5

Some things that I want to cover with my therapist in our next session. These can be related to the main reason(s) you are going to therapy, other issue(s), or something completely unrelated about which you would like to speak to your therapist.

_____

_____

_____

_____

_____

"You gain strength, courage, and confidence by every experience in which you really stop and look fear in the face." Eleanor Roosevelt

After 3rd session

What we talked about in our therapy session:

_____

_____

_____

_____

_____

Main items or ideas that stand out from today's session:

_____

_____

_____

_____

Key things I need to work on this week include:

_____

_____

_____

_____

_____

Take a moment to revisit these two questions:

1. Do I feel a rapport and trust between myself and my therapist? Has this grown or diminished over the few session we've had?

_____

_____

_____

_____

_____

2. Do I feel that this therapist is helping me with my problem(s)?

_____

_____

_____

_____

_____

If you are sensing issues with either of these two questions, write them in the "Prior to 4th session : Some things that I want to cover with my therapist in our next session" section.

Rate how you are feeling about the main areas of your life:

Work.

1   2   3   4   5   6   7   8   9   10
(low)   (neutral)   (optimal)

Leisure

1   2   3   4   5   6   7   8   9   10

Social

1   2   3   4   5   6   7   8   9   10

Sexual

1   2   3   4   5   6   7   8   9   10

Being with myself

1   2   3   4   5   6   7   8   9   10

Spirituality

1   2   3   4   5   6   7   8   9   10

"As soon as you trust yourself, you will know how to live."—Johann von Goethe

Prior to 4th session

Dreams I had this week (remember to also write how you felt upon waking from each dream).

_____

_____

_____

_____

_____

Experiences I had this week that teach me specific lessons about myself.

_____

_____

_____

_____

_____

Now shift to the problem(s) that you are working on in therapy. Write out how you are doing with those problem(s) this week.

_____

_____

_____

_____

_____

Write out how your problem(s) have changed through your first 3 therapy sessions.

_____

_____

_____

_____

_____

Write out how you would like your problem(s) to continue changing.

_____

_____

_____

_____

_____

This section allows you to "free associate", writing whatever comes to your mind. You may answer the statement directly, write whatever comes to mind after reading the statement, or simply write whatever you like–even if it's simply what you are thinking and feeling.

One or two things that I really want right now are...

_____

_____

_____

_____

_____

Some things that I want to cover with my therapist in our next session. These can be related to the main reason(s) you are going to therapy, other issue(s), or something completely unrelated about which you would like to speak to your therapist.

_____

_____

_____

_____

_____

"Human beings, by changing the inner attitudes of their minds, can change the outer aspects of their lives."—William James

After 4th session

What we talked about in our therapy session:

_____

_____

_____

_____

_____

Main items or ideas that stand out from today's session:

_____

_____

_____

_____

_____

Key things I need to work on this week include:

_____

_____

_____

_____

_____

Important insights I am finding out about myself:

_____

_____

_____

_____

_____

Rate how you are feeling about the main areas of your life:

Work.

1	2	3	4	5	6	7	8	9	10
(low)				(neutral)				(optimal)	

Leisure

| 1 | 2 | 3 | 4 | 5 | 6 | 7 | 8 | 9 | 10 |

Social

| 1 | 2 | 3 | 4 | 5 | 6 | 7 | 8 | 9 | 10 |

Sexual

| 1 | 2 | 3 | 4 | 5 | 6 | 7 | 8 | 9 | 10 |

Being with myself

| 1 | 2 | 3 | 4 | 5 | 6 | 7 | 8 | 9 | 10 |

Spirituality

| 1 | 2 | 3 | 4 | 5 | 6 | 7 | 8 | 9 | 10 |

"A moment's insight is sometimes worth a life's experience."–Oliver Wendell Holmes

Prior to 5th session

Dreams I had this week (remember to also write how you felt upon waking from each dream).

_____

_____

_____

_____

_____

Experiences I had this week that teach me specific lessons about myself.

_____

_____

_____

_____

_____

Now shift to the problem(s) that you are working on in therapy. Write out how you are doing with those problem(s) this week.

_____

_____

_____

_____

_____

Most psychological disorders have an underlying (unconscious) goal behind them. For example, someone may experience a depression in order to feel weak enough not to work. Think about your current problem(s), and what may be some of your underlying goals.

_____

_____

_____

_____

_____

"Free association" section. You may answer the following statement directly, write whatever comes to mind after reading the statement, or simply write whatever you like–even if it's simply what you are thinking and feeling.

I am not currently living my life to its full potential…

_____

_____

_____

_____

_____

Some things that I want to cover with my therapist in our next session. These can be related to the main reason(s) you are going to therapy, other issue(s), or something completely unrelated about which you would like to speak to your therapist.

_____

_____

_____

_____

_____

"Every psychological activity shows that its direction is governed by a predetermined goal."—Alfred Adler

After 5th session

What we talked about in our therapy session:

_____

_____

_____

_____

_____

Main items or ideas that stand out from today's session:

_____

_____

_____

_____

_____

Key things I need to work on this week include:

_____

_____

_____

_____

_____

The most important thing that my therapist has taught me so far is:

_____

_____

_____

_____

_____

Rate how you are feeling about the main areas of your life:

Work.

| 1 | 2 | 3 | 4 | 5 | 6 | 7 | 8 | 9 | 10 |
| (low) | | | | (neutral) | | | | (optimal) | |

Leisure

| 1 | 2 | 3 | 4 | 5 | 6 | 7 | 8 | 9 | 10 |

Social

| 1 | 2 | 3 | 4 | 5 | 6 | 7 | 8 | 9 | 10 |

Sexual

| 1 | 2 | 3 | 4 | 5 | 6 | 7 | 8 | 9 | 10 |

Being with myself

| 1 | 2 | 3 | 4 | 5 | 6 | 7 | 8 | 9 | 10 |

Spirituality

| 1 | 2 | 3 | 4 | 5 | 6 | 7 | 8 | 9 | 10 |

Take some time to consider how your ratings have changed over the past few weeks. Optimally, what would you like these ratings to be?

Work.
1   2   3   4   5   6   7   8   9   10
(low)   (neutral)   (optimal)

Leisure

1   2   3   4   5   6   7   8   9   10

Social

1   2   3   4   5   6   7   8   9   10

Sexual

1   2   3   4   5   6   7   8   9   10

Being with myself

1   2   3   4   5   6   7   8   9   10

Spirituality

1   2   3   4   5   6   7   8   9   10

How do you feel about these "ratings goals"? What would you like to do in order to achieve them?

_____
_____
_____
_____
_____

"The indispensable first step to getting the things you want out of life is this : decide what you want."—Ben Stein

Prior to 6ᵗʰ session

Dreams I had this week (remember to also write how you felt upon waking from each dream).

_____

_____

_____

_____

_____

Experiences I had this week that teach me specific lessons about myself.

_____

_____

_____

_____

_____

Take some time to think about your interactions with family and friends. Write about how they have evolved now that you are in therapy.

_____

_____

_____

_____

_____

Now shift to the problem(s) that you are working on in therapy. Write out how you are doing with those problem(s) this week.

_____

_____

_____

_____

_____

"Free association" section. You may answer the following statement directly, write whatever comes to mind after reading the statement, or simply write whatever you like–even if it's simply what you are thinking and feeling.

One or two things that I am really good at are…

_____

_____

_____

_____

_____

Some things that I want to cover with my therapist in our next session. These can be related to the main reason(s) you are going to therapy, other issue(s), or something completely unrelated about which you would like to speak to your therapist.

_____

_____

_____

_____

_____

"Everything that irritates us about others can lead us to an understanding of ourselves."—Carl Jung

After 6th session

What we talked about in our therapy session:

_____

_____

_____

_____

_____

Main items or ideas that stand out from today's session:

_____

_____

_____

_____

_____

Key things I need to work on this week include:

_____

_____

_____

_____

_____

If I could write a 2-3 line summary of my therapy so far, it would include the following.

_____

_____

_____

_____

_____

Rate how you are feeling about the main areas of your life:

Work.

1   2   3   4   5   6   7   8   9   10
(low)   (neutral)   (optimal)

Leisure

1   2   3   4   5   6   7   8   9   10

Social

1   2   3   4   5   6   7   8   9   10

Sexual

1   2   3   4   5   6   7   8   9   10

Being with myself

1   2   3   4   5   6   7   8   9   10

Spirituality

1   2   3   4   5   6   7   8   9   10

"Many of life's failures are people who did not realize how close they were to success when they gave up."—Thomas Edison

Prior to 7th session

Dreams I had this week (remember to also write how you felt upon waking from each dream).

_____

_____

_____

_____

_____

Experiences I had this week that teach me specific lessons about myself.

_____

_____

_____

_____

_____

Take a moment to write about some of your hobbies, and/or some things that you might like to become hobbies.

_____

_____

_____

_____

_____

Now shift to the problem(s) that you are working on in therapy. Write out how you are doing with those problem(s) this week.

_____

_____

_____

_____

_____

This section allows you to "free associate", writing whatever comes to your mind. You may answer the statement directly, write whatever comes to mind after reading the statement, or simply write whatever you like–even if it's simply what you are thinking and feeling.

These are some things I really enjoy…

_____

_____

_____

_____

_____

Some things that I want to cover with my therapist in our next session. These can be related to the main reason(s) you are going to therapy, other issue(s), or something completely unrelated about which you would like to speak to your therapist.

_____

_____

_____

_____

_____

"I think, therefore I am."—Rene Descartes

After 7th session

What we talked about in our therapy session:

_____
_____
_____
_____
_____

Main items or ideas that stand out from today's session:

_____
_____
_____
_____

Key things I need to work on this week include:

_____
_____
_____
_____
_____

Right now, this is how I'm feeling "in general":

_____
_____
_____
_____
_____

Rate how you are feeling about the main areas of your life:

Work.

1   2   3   4   5   6   7   8   9   10
(low)   (neutral)   (optimal)

Leisure

1   2   3   4   5   6   7   8   9   10

Social

1   2   3   4   5   6   7   8   9   10

Sexual

1   2   3   4   5   6   7   8   9   10

Being with myself

1   2   3   4   5   6   7   8   9   10

Spirituality

1   2   3   4   5   6   7   8   9   10

Take some time to consider how your ratings have changed over the past two weeks. What can you do, or continue doing, for these ratings to become closer to your "ratings goals"? (If this question causes tension or anxiety, why?)

_____

_____

_____

_____

_____

"Don't fear failure so much that you refuse to try new things. The saddest summary of a life contains three descriptions : could have, might have, and should have."—Louis E. Boone

Prior to 8th session

Dreams I had this week (remember to also write how you felt upon waking from each dream).

_____

_____

_____

_____

_____

Experiences I had this week that teach me specific lessons about myself.

_____

_____

_____

_____

Some things that make me feel very safe and secure (and why) are:

_____

_____

_____

_____

_____

Now shift to the problem(s) that you are working on in therapy. Write out how you are doing with those problem(s) this week.

_____

_____

_____

_____

_____

"Free association" section. You may answer the following statement directly, write whatever comes to mind after reading the statement, or simply write whatever you like–even if it's simply what you are thinking and feeling.

Some of my lifelong dreams are…

_____

_____

_____

_____

_____

Some things that I want to cover with my therapist in our next session. These can be related to the main reason(s) you are going to therapy, other issue(s), or something completely unrelated about which you would like to speak to your therapist.

_____

_____

_____

_____

_____

"To accomplish great things, we must dream as well as act."—Anatole France

After 8th session

What we talked about in our therapy session:

_____
_____
_____
_____
_____

Main items or ideas that stand out from today's session:

_____
_____
_____
_____
_____

Key things I need to work on this week include:

_____
_____
_____
_____
_____

Some things that my therapist might have learned from me are:

_____
_____
_____
_____
_____

Rate how you are feeling about the main areas of your life:

Work.

1   2   3   4   5   6   7   8   9   10
(low)   (neutral)   (optimal)

Leisure

1   2   3   4   5   6   7   8   9   10

Social

1   2   3   4   5   6   7   8   9   10

Sexual

1   2   3   4   5   6   7   8   9   10

Being with myself

1   2   3   4   5   6   7   8   9   10

Spirituality

1   2   3   4   5   6   7   8   9   10

"There are three ingredients to the good life : learning, earning, and yearning."—Christopher Morley

Prior to 9th session

Dreams I had this week (remember to also write how you felt upon waking from each dream).

_____
_____
_____
_____
_____

Experiences I had this week that teach me specific lessons about myself.

_____
_____
_____
_____
_____

If I were a painter, this is what I would like to paint:

_____
_____
_____
_____
_____

Now shift to the problem(s) that you are working on in therapy. Write out how you are doing with those problem(s) this week.

_____

_____

_____

_____

_____

"Free association" section. You may answer the following statement directly, write whatever comes to mind after reading the statement, or simply write whatever you like–even if it's simply what you are thinking and feeling.

What growth means to me is…

_____

_____

_____

_____

_____

Some things that I want to cover with my therapist in our next session. These can be related to the main reason(s) you are going to therapy, other issue(s), or something completely unrelated about which you would like to speak to your therapist.

_____

_____

_____

_____

_____

"With every experience, you alone are painting your own canvas, thought by thought, choice by choice."—Oprah Winfrey

After 9th session

What we talked about in our therapy session:

_____

_____

_____

_____

_____

Main items or ideas that stand out from today's session:

_____

_____

_____

_____

_____

Key things I need to work on this week include:

_____

_____

_____

_____

_____

"Free Section". In this section, please feel free to journal about whatever you want. Thoughts you had or are having, feelings you had or are having, or anything else you would like to journal.

_____

_____

_____

_____

_____

Rate how you are feeling about the main areas of your life:

Work.

1   2   3   4   5   6   7   8   9   10
(low)   (neutral)   (optimal)

Leisure

1   2   3   4   5   6   7   8   9   10

Social

1   2   3   4   5   6   7   8   9   10

Sexual

1   2   3   4   5   6   7   8   9   10

Being with myself

1   2   3   4   5   6   7   8   9   10

Spirituality

1   2   3   4   5   6   7   8   9   10

Take some time to consider how your ratings have changed over the past two weeks. What can you do, or continue doing, for these ratings to become closer to your "ratings goals"? (If this question causes tension or anxiety, why?)

_____

_____

_____

_____

_____

"The best and safest thing is to keep a balance in your life, acknowledge the great powers around us and in us."—Euripides

Prior to 10th session

Dreams I had this week (remember to also write how you felt upon waking from each dream).

_____

_____

_____

_____

_____

Experiences I had this week that teach me specific lessons about myself.

_____

_____

_____

_____

_____

Take some time to think about your relationships in general. Write about how they are changing now that you are in therapy.

_____

_____

_____

_____

_____

Now shift to the problem(s) that you are working on in therapy. Write out how you are doing with those problem(s) this week.

_____

_____

_____

_____

_____

"Free association" section. You may answer the following statement directly, write whatever comes to mind after reading the statement, or simply write whatever you like–even if it's simply what you are thinking and feeling.

I am remarkable in the following ways…

_____

_____

_____

_____

_____

Some things that I want to cover with my therapist in our next session. These can be related to the main reason(s) you are going to therapy, other issue(s), or something completely unrelated about which you would like to speak to your therapist.

_____

_____

_____

_____

_____

"Treasure your relationships, not your possessions."—Anthony D'Angelo

After 10th session

What we talked about in our therapy session:

_____
_____
_____
_____
_____

Main items or ideas that stand out from today's session:

_____
_____
_____
_____
_____

Key things I need to work on this week include:

_____
_____
_____
_____
_____

"Free Section". In this section, please feel free to journal about whatever you want. Thoughts you had or are having, feelings you had or are having, or anything else you would like to journal. You also may continue what you started to write about in last week's "free section" if you so choose.

_____

_____

_____

_____

_____

Rate how you are feeling about the main areas of your life:

Work.

1	2	3	4	5	6	7	8	9	10
(low)				(neutral)				(optimal)	

Leisure

1 2 3 4 5 6 7 8 9 10

Social

1 2 3 4 5 6 7 8 9 10

Sexual

1 2 3 4 5 6 7 8 9 10

Being with myself

1 2 3 4 5 6 7 8 9 10

Spirituality

1 2 3 4 5 6 7 8 9 10

"I want freedom for the full expression of my personality."—Mahatma Ghandi

Prior to 11th session

Dreams I had this week (remember to also write how you felt upon waking from each dream).

_____

_____

_____

_____

_____

Experiences I had this week that teach me specific lessons about myself.

_____

_____

_____

_____

_____

Take some time to think about how others view you. Write about those views, and how you feel about them.

_____

_____

_____

_____

Now shift to the problem(s) that you are working on in therapy. Write out how you are doing with those problem(s) this week.

_____

_____

_____

_____

_____

"Free association" section. You may answer the following statement directly, write whatever comes to mind after reading the statement, or simply write whatever you like–even if it's simply what you are thinking and feeling.

I am me…

_____

_____

_____

_____

_____

Some things that I want to cover with my therapist in our next session. These can be related to the main reason(s) you are going to therapy, other issue(s), or something completely unrelated about which you would like to speak to your therapist.

_____

_____

_____

_____

_____

"Men [and women] acquire a particular quality by constantly acting a particular way…you become just by performing just actions, temperate by performing temperate actions, brave by performing brave actions."—Aristotle

After 11th session

What we talked about in our therapy session:

_____

_____

_____

_____

_____

Main items or ideas that stand out from today's session:

_____

_____

_____

_____

_____

Key things I need to work on this week include:

_____

_____

_____

_____

_____

"Free Section". In this section, please feel free to journal about whatever you want. Thoughts you had or are having, feelings you had or are having, or anything else you would like to journal. You also may continue what you started to write about in last week's "free section" if you so choose.

_____

_____

_____

_____

_____

Rate how you are feeling about the main areas of your life:

Work.

1   2   3   4   5   6   7   8   9   10
(low)   (neutral)   (optimal)

Leisure

1   2   3   4   5   6   7   8   9   10

Social

1   2   3   4   5   6   7   8   9   10

Sexual

1   2   3   4   5   6   7   8   9   10

Being with myself

1   2   3   4   5   6   7   8   9   10

Spirituality

1   2   3   4   5   6   7   8   9   10

Take some time to consider how your ratings have changed over the past two weeks. What can you do, or continue doing, for these ratings to become closer to your "ratings goals"?

_____

_____

_____

_____

_____

"Let me tell you the secret that has led me to my goal. My strength lies solely in my tenacity."—Louis Pasteur

Prior to 12th session

Dreams I had this week (remember to also write how you felt upon waking from each dream).

_____

_____

_____

_____

_____

Experiences I had this week that teach me specific lessons about myself.

_____

_____

_____

_____

If you had a garden that was a reflection of yourself, what would be in that garden and how would it be arranged? How has your garden changed over this past year?

_____

_____

_____

_____

_____

Now shift to the problem(s) that you are working on in therapy. Write out how you are doing with those problem(s) this week.

_____
_____
_____
_____
_____

"Free association" section. You may answer the following statement directly, write whatever comes to mind after reading the statement, or simply write whatever you like–even if it's simply what you are thinking and feeling.

Some of my strengths are…

_____
_____
_____
_____

Some things that I want to cover with my therapist in our next session. These can be related to the main reason(s) you are going to therapy, other issue(s), or something completely unrelated about which you would like to speak to your therapist.

_____
_____
_____
_____
_____

"Our bodies are our gardens to which our wills are our gardeners."—William Shakespeare

After 12th session

What we talked about in our therapy session:

_____
_____
_____
_____
_____

Main items or ideas that stand out from today's session:

_____
_____
_____
_____
_____

Key things I need to work on this week include:

_____
_____
_____
_____
_____

"Free Section". In this section, please feel free to journal about whatever you want.

_____

_____

_____

_____

_____

Rate how you are feeling about the main areas of your life:

Work.

1   2   3   4   5   6   7   8   9   10
(low)   (neutral)   (optimal)

Leisure

1   2   3   4   5   6   7   8   9   10

Social

1   2   3   4   5   6   7   8   9   10

Sexual

1   2   3   4   5   6   7   8   9   10

Being with myself

1   2   3   4   5   6   7   8   9   10

Spirituality

1   2   3   4   5   6   7   8   9   10

"Enjoy your own life without comparing it with that of another."—Marquis de Condorcet

Prior to 13th session

Dreams I had this week (remember to also write how you felt upon waking from each dream).

_____

_____

_____

_____

_____

Experiences I had this week that teach me specific lessons about myself.

_____

_____

_____

_____

_____

What does the number 13 mean to you?

_____

_____

_____

_____

_____

Now shift to the problem(s) that you are working on in therapy. Write out how you are doing with those problem(s) this week.

_____

_____

_____

_____

_____

"Free association" section. You may answer the following statement directly, write whatever comes to mind after reading the statement, or simply write whatever you like–even if it's simply what you are thinking and feeling.

We are all in this journey of life together...

_____

_____

_____

_____

_____

Some things that I want to cover with my therapist in our next session. These can be related to the main reason(s) you are going to therapy, other issue(s), or something completely unrelated about which you would like to speak to your therapist.

_____

_____

_____

_____

_____

"I'm a great believer in luck, and I find the harder I work the more I have of it."—Thomas Jefferson

After 13th session

What we talked about in our therapy session:

_____
_____
_____
_____
_____

Main items or ideas that stand out from today's session:

_____
_____
_____
_____
_____

Key things I need to work on this week include:

_____
_____
_____
_____
_____

"Free Section". In this section, please feel free to journal about whatever you want.

_____

_____

_____

_____

_____

Rate how you are feeling about the main areas of your life:

Work.

| 1 | 2 | 3 | 4 | 5 | 6 | 7 | 8 | 9 | 10 |
(low)   (neutral)   (optimal)

Leisure

1   2   3   4   5   6   7   8   9   10

Social

1   2   3   4   5   6   7   8   9   10

Sexual

1   2   3   4   5   6   7   8   9   10

Being with myself

1   2   3   4   5   6   7   8   9   10

Spirituality

1   2   3   4   5   6   7   8   9   10

Take some time to consider how your ratings have changed over the past two weeks. What would you like to continue doing for these ratings to become closer to your "ratings goals"? What would you like to change in order for these ratings to become closer to your "ratings goals"?

_____

_____

_____

_____

_____

"You always pass failure on the way to success."—Mickey Rooney

Prior to 14th session

Dreams I had this week (remember to also write how you felt upon waking from each dream).

_____
_____
_____
_____
_____

Experiences I had this week that teach me specific lessons about myself.

_____
_____
_____
_____
_____

Take some time to think about your life in general. Write about how it is evolving through your therapy.

_____
_____
_____
_____
_____

Now shift to the problem(s) that you are working on in therapy. Write out how you are doing with those problem(s) this week.

_____

_____

_____

_____

_____

"Free association" section. You may answer the following statement directly, write whatever comes to mind after reading the statement, or simply write whatever you like–even if it's simply what you are thinking and feeling.

Deep down, I really want…

_____

_____

_____

_____

_____

Some things that I want to cover with my therapist in our next session. These can be related to the main reason(s) you are going to therapy, other issue(s), or something completely unrelated about which you would like to speak to your therapist.

_____

_____

_____

_____

_____

"Everything has its beauty but not everyone sees it."—Confucius

After 14th session

What we talked about in our therapy session:

_____

_____

_____

_____

_____

Main items or ideas that stand out from today's session:

_____

_____

_____

_____

Key things I need to work on this week include:

_____

_____

_____

_____

"Free Section". In this section, please feel free to journal about whatever you want.

_____
_____
_____
_____
_____

Rate how you are feeling about the main areas of your life:

Work.

1   2   3   4   5   6   7   8   9   10
(low)   (neutral)   (optimal)

Leisure

1   2   3   4   5   6   7   8   9   10

Social

1   2   3   4   5   6   7   8   9   10

Sexual

1   2   3   4   5   6   7   8   9   10

Being with myself

1   2   3   4   5   6   7   8   9   10

Spirituality

1   2   3   4   5   6   7   8   9   10

"The greatest gift is not found in a store nor under a tree, but in the hearts of true friends."—Cindy Lew

Prior to 15th session

Dreams I had this week (remember to also write how you felt upon waking from each dream).

_____
_____
_____
_____
_____

Experiences I had this week that teach me specific lessons about myself.

_____
_____
_____
_____
_____

Write a short poem from your heart.

_____
_____
_____
_____
_____

Now shift to the problem(s) that you are working on in therapy. Write out how you are doing with those problem(s) this week.

_____

_____

_____

_____

_____

"Free association" section. You may answer the following statement directly, write whatever comes to mind after reading the statement, or simply write whatever you like–even if it's simply what you are thinking and feeling.

I am enjoying this moment...

_____

_____

_____

_____

_____

Some things that I want to cover with my therapist in our next session. These can be related to the main reason(s) you are going to therapy, other issue(s), or something completely unrelated about which you would like to speak to your therapist.

_____

_____

_____

_____

_____

"Genuine poetry can communicate before it is understood."—T.S. Eliot

After 15th session

What we talked about in our therapy session:

_____

_____

_____

_____

_____

Main items or ideas that stand out from today's session:

_____

_____

_____

_____

_____

Key things I need to work on this week include:

_____

_____

_____

_____

_____

"Free Section". In this section, please feel free to journal about whatever you want.

_____

_____

_____

_____

_____

Rate how you are feeling about the main areas of your life:

Work.

1   2   3   4   5   6   7   8   9   10
(low)   (neutral)   (optimal)

Leisure

1   2   3   4   5   6   7   8   9   10

Social

1   2   3   4   5   6   7   8   9   10

Sexual

1   2   3   4   5   6   7   8   9   10

Being with myself

1   2   3   4   5   6   7   8   9   10

Spirituality

1   2   3   4   5   6   7   8   9   10

Take some time to consider how your ratings have changed over the past two weeks. What would you like to continue doing for these ratings to become closer to your "ratings goals"? What would you like to change in order for these ratings to become closer to your "ratings goals"?

_____

_____

_____

_____

_____

"Every day you make progress. Every step may be fruitful. Yet there will stretch out before you an ever-lengthening, ever-ascending, every-improving path. You know you will never get to the end of the journey. But this, so far from discouraging, only adds to the joy and glory of the climb."—Sir Winston Churchill

Prior to 16th session

Dreams I had this week (remember to also write how you felt upon waking from each dream).

_____

_____

_____

_____

_____

Experiences I had this week that teach me specific lessons about myself.

_____

_____

_____

_____

Draw a picture about whatever comes to your mind.

Now shift to the problem(s) that you are working on in therapy. Write out how you are doing with those problem(s) this week.

_____
_____
_____
_____
_____

"Free association" section. You may answer the following statement directly, write whatever comes to mind after reading the statement, or simply write whatever you like–even if it's simply what you are thinking and feeling.

Life is a gift…

_____
_____
_____
_____
_____

Some things that I want to cover with my therapist in our next session. These can be related to the main reason(s) you are going to therapy, other issue(s), or something completely unrelated about which you would like to speak to your therapist.

_____
_____
_____
_____
_____

"Art is a collaboration between God and the artist, and the less the artist does the better."—Andre Gide

After 16th session

What we talked about in our therapy session:

_____

_____

_____

_____

_____

Main items or ideas that stand out from today's session:

_____

_____

_____

_____

_____

Key things I need to work on this week include:

_____

_____

_____

_____

_____

"Free Section". In this section, please feel free to journal about whatever you want.

_____

_____

_____

_____

_____

Rate how you are feeling about the main areas of your life:

Work.
1   2   3   4   5   6   7   8   9   10
(low)   (neutral)   (optimal)

Leisure

1   2   3   4   5   6   7   8   9   10

Social

1   2   3   4   5   6   7   8   9   10

Sexual

1   2   3   4   5   6   7   8   9   10

Being with myself

1   2   3   4   5   6   7   8   9   10

Spirituality

1   2   3   4   5   6   7   8   9   10

"True silence is the rest of the mind; it is to the spirit what sleep is to the body, nourishment and refreshment."—William Penn

Prior to 17th session

Dreams I had this week (remember to also write how you felt upon waking from each dream).

_____
_____
_____
_____
_____

Experiences I had this week that teach me specific lessons about myself.

_____
_____
_____
_____
_____

Write about your favorite book, movie, or TV show. Who is your favorite character and why?

_____
_____
_____
_____
_____

Now shift to the problem(s) that you are working on in therapy. Write out how you are doing with those problem(s) this week.

_____

_____

_____

_____

_____

"Free association" section. You may answer the following statement directly, write whatever comes to mind after reading the statement, or simply write whatever you like–even if it's simply what you are thinking and feeling.

I feel happy about…

_____

_____

_____

_____

_____

Some things that I want to cover with my therapist in our next session. These can be related to the main reason(s) you are going to therapy, other issue(s), or something completely unrelated about which you would like to speak to your therapist.

_____

_____

_____

_____

_____

"My favorite thing is to go where I've never been."—Diane Arbus

After 17th session

What we talked about in our therapy session:

_____
_____
_____
_____
_____

Main items or ideas that stand out from today's session:

_____
_____
_____
_____
_____

Key things I need to work on this week include:

_____
_____
_____
_____
_____

"Free Section". In this section, please feel free to journal about whatever you want.

_____

_____

_____

_____

_____

Rate how you are feeling about the main areas of your life:

Work.
1   2   3   4   5   6   7   8   9   10
(low)   (neutral)   (optimal)

Leisure

1   2   3   4   5   6   7   8   9   10

Social

1   2   3   4   5   6   7   8   9   10

Sexual

1   2   3   4   5   6   7   8   9   10

Being with myself

1   2   3   4   5   6   7   8   9   10

Spirituality

1   2   3   4   5   6   7   8   9   10

Take some time to consider how your ratings have changed over the past two weeks. What would you like to continue doing for these ratings to become closer to your "ratings goals"? What would you like to change in order for these ratings to become closer to your "ratings goals"?

_____

_____

_____

_____

_____

"The greatest discovery of my generation is that a human being can alter his life by altering his attitude."—William James

Prior to 18th session

Dreams I had this week (remember to also write how you felt upon waking from each dream).

_____

_____

_____

_____

_____

Experiences I had this week that teach me specific lessons about myself.

_____

_____

_____

_____

_____

Now shift to the problem(s) that you are working on in therapy. Write out how you are doing with those problem(s) this week.

_____

_____

_____

_____

On a scale of 1 (lowest) to 5 (highest), how well am I overcoming these problems?

1   2   3   4   5

On a scale of 1 (lowest) to 5 (highest), how well does my therapist feel I am overcoming these problems?

1   2   3   4   5

"Free association" section. You may answer the following statement directly, write whatever comes to mind after reading the statement, or simply write whatever you like–even if it's simply what you are thinking and feeling.

I love…

_____

_____

_____

_____

_____

Some things that I want to cover with my therapist in our next session. These can be related to the main reason(s) you are going to therapy, other issue(s), or something completely unrelated about which you would like to speak to your therapist.

_____

_____

_____

_____

_____

"Although the world is full of suffering, it is full also of the overcoming of it."—Helen Keller

After 18th session

What we talked about in our therapy session:

_____
_____
_____
_____
_____

Main items or ideas that stand out from today's session:

_____
_____
_____
_____
_____

Key things I need to work on this week include:

_____
_____
_____
_____
_____

"Free Section". In this section, please feel free to journal about whatever you want.

_____

_____

_____

_____

_____

Rate how you are feeling about the main areas of your life:

Work.

1   2   3   4   5   6   7   8   9   10
(low)   (neutral)   (optimal)

Leisure

1   2   3   4   5   6   7   8   9   10

Social

1   2   3   4   5   6   7   8   9   10

Sexual

1   2   3   4   5   6   7   8   9   10

Being with myself

1   2   3   4   5   6   7   8   9   10

Spirituality

1   2   3   4   5   6   7   8   9   10

"Our feelings are our most genuine paths to knowledge."—Andre Lorde

Prior to 19th session

Dreams I had this week (remember to also write how you felt upon waking from each dream).

_____

_____

_____

_____

_____

Experiences I had this week that teach me specific lessons about myself.

_____

_____

_____

_____

_____

Now shift to the problem(s) that you are working on in therapy. Write out how you are doing with those problem(s) this week.

_____

_____

_____

_____

_____

On a scale of 1 (lowest) to 5 (highest), how well am I overcoming these problems?

1   2   3   4   5

On a scale of 1 (lowest) to 5 (highest), how well does my therapist feel I am overcoming these problems?

1   2   3   4   5

"Free association" section. You may answer the following statement directly, write whatever comes to mind after reading the statement, or simply write whatever you like–even if it's simply what you are thinking and feeling.

The best vacation I ever took was (or could imagine taking is)…

_____

_____

_____

_____

_____

Some things that I want to cover with my therapist in our next session. These can be related to the main reason(s) you are going to therapy, other issue(s), or something completely unrelated about which you would like to speak to your therapist.

_____

_____

_____

_____

_____

"Take a chance! All life is a chance. The man [or woman] who goes furthest is generally the one who is willing to do and dare."—Dale Carnegie

After 19th session

What we talked about in our therapy session:

_____
_____
_____
_____
_____

Main items or ideas that stand out from today's session:

_____
_____
_____
_____
_____

Key things I need to work on this week include:

_____
_____
_____
_____
_____

"Free Section". In this section, please feel free to journal about whatever you want. Thoughts you had or are having, feelings you had or are having, or anything else you would like to journal.

_____

_____

_____

_____

_____

Rate how you are feeling about the main areas of your life:

Work.

1   2   3   4   5   6   7   8   9   10
(low)   (neutral)   (optimal)

Leisure

1   2   3   4   5   6   7   8   9   10

Social

1   2   3   4   5   6   7   8   9   10

Sexual

1   2   3   4   5   6   7   8   9   10

Being with myself

1   2   3   4   5   6   7   8   9   10

Spirituality

1   2   3   4   5   6   7   8   9   10

Take some time to consider how your ratings have changed over the past two weeks. As this journal begins to conclude, what would you like to do for these ratings to become closer to your "ratings goals"?

_____

_____

_____

_____

_____

"It's easy to survive, but difficult to really live."—J. Slava Thaler

Prior to 20th session

Dreams I had this week (remember to also write how you felt upon waking from each dream).

_____

_____ _____

_____

_____

_____

Experiences I had this week that teach me specific lessons about myself.

_____

_____

_____

_____

Now shift to the problem(s) that you are working on in therapy. Write out how you are doing with those problem(s) this week.

_____

_____

_____

_____

On a scale of 1 (lowest) to 5 (highest), how well am I overcoming these problems?

1   2   3   4   5

On a scale of 1 (lowest) to 5 (highest), how well does my therapist feel I am over-coming these problems?

1   2   3   4   5

"Free association" section. You may answer the following statement directly, write whatever comes to mind after reading the statement, or simply write whatever you like–even if it's simply what you are thinking and feeling.

When I think of completion, I think and feel...

_____
_____
_____
_____
_____

Some things that I want to cover with my therapist in our next session. These can be related to the main reason(s) you are going to therapy, other issue(s), or something completely unrelated about which you would like to speak to your therapist.

_____
_____
_____
_____
_____

"The first principle is that you must not fool yourself–and you are the easiest person to fool."—Richard Feynman

After 20th session

What we talked about in our therapy session:

_____

_____

_____

_____

_____

Main items or ideas that stand out from today's session:

_____

_____

_____

_____

_____

Key things I need to work on this week include:

_____

_____

_____

_____

_____

If I could write a synopsis of my therapy so far, it would include the following.

_____

_____

_____

_____

_____

"Free Section". In this section, please feel free to journal about whatever you want. Thoughts you had or are having, feelings you had or are having, or anything else you would like to journal.

_____

_____

_____

_____

_____

Rate how you are feeling about the main areas of your life:

Work.

1   2   3   4   5   6   7   8   9   10
(low)   (neutral)   (optimal)

Leisure

1   2   3   4   5   6   7   8   9   10

Social

1   2   3   4   5   6   7   8   9   10

Sexual

1   2   3   4   5   6   7   8   9   10

Being with myself

1   2   3   4   5   6   7   8   9   10

Spirituality

1   2   3   4   5   6   7   8   9   10

Take some time to consider how you feel about your ratings today. How do you want to move forward?

_____

_____

_____

_____

_____

"It requires great courage to preserve inner freedom, to move on in one's inward journey into new realms."—Rollo May

About the Author

J. Slava Thaler is a psychotherapist in private practice. He holds a Masters Degree in Counseling Psychology, and a Doctorate in Alternative Medicines. He was formerly the President & CEO of ReachApex, Inc. You may contact J. Slava Thaler about speaking engagements by emailing slava@mnhelp.com.

0-595-30857-0